OUR
FAMILY
TRADITIONS

Moments, milestones
& memories

CHRONICLE BOOKS
SAN FRANCISCO

OUR FAMILY TREE

GREAT-GRANDPARENT

GREAT-GRANDPARENT

GREAT-GRANDPARENT

GREAT-GRANDPARENT

GRANDPARENT

GRANDPARENT

PARENT

CHILDREN

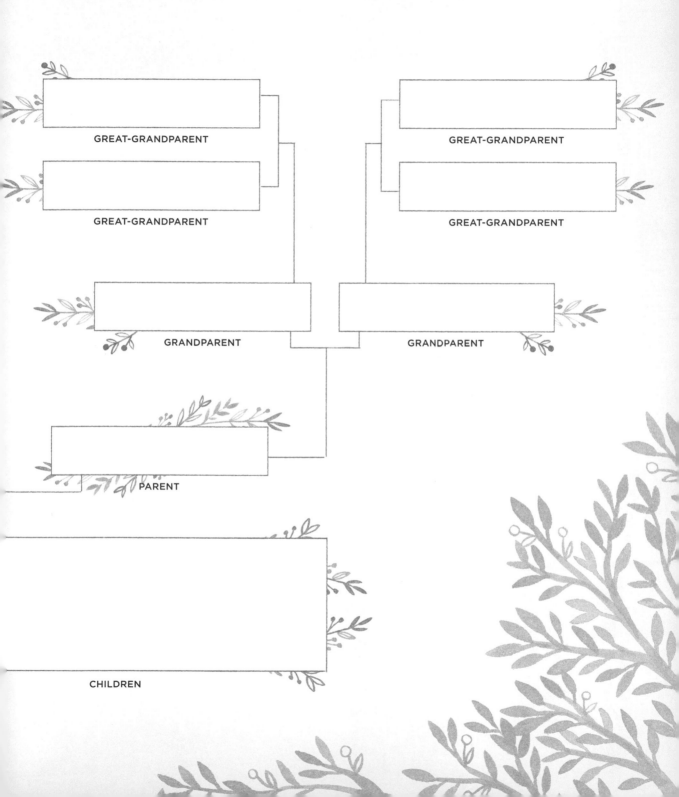

GREAT-GRANDPARENT

GREAT-GRANDPARENT

GREAT-GRANDPARENT

GREAT-GRANDPARENT

GRANDPARENT

GRANDPARENT

PARENT

CHILDREN

ABOUT OUR

FAMILY

OUR FAMILY TIMELINE

Mark off momentous moments and cherished memories,
such as new births or big moves.

**WHEN WE
BECAME
A FAMILY**

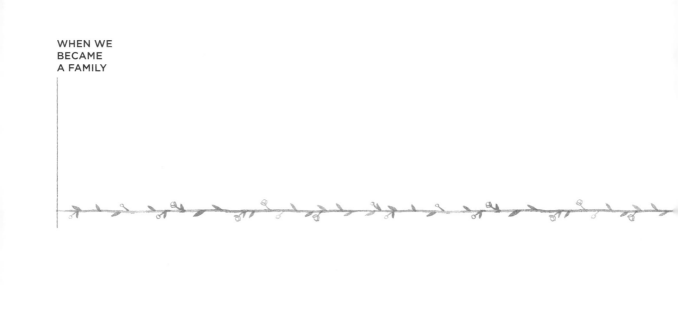

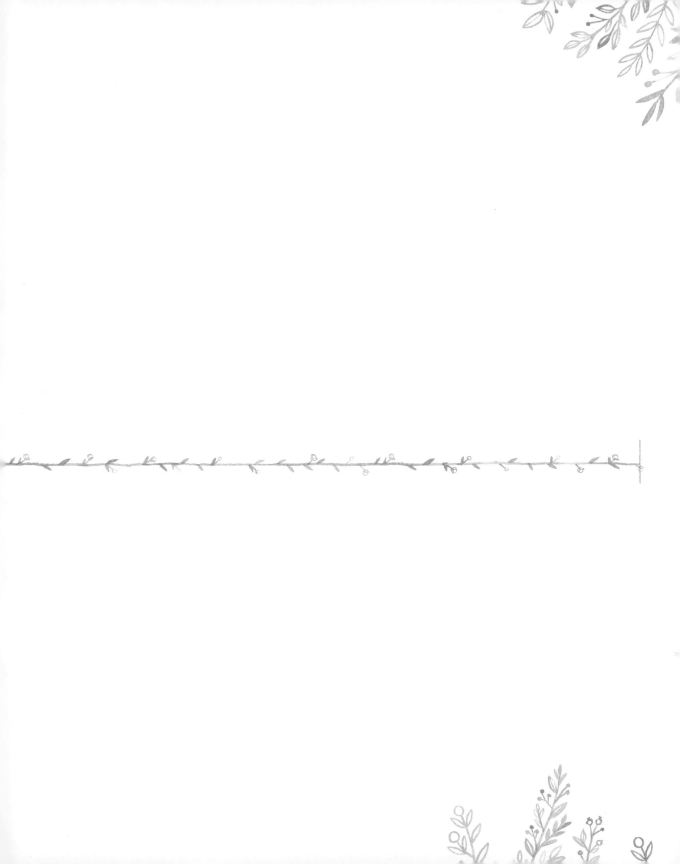

MEMBERS OF OUR FAMILY

_____
NAME

_____
NICKNAME(S)

_____
BIRTHDAY

_____
PERSON I AM NAMED AFTER

_____
WHO I LOOK LIKE

_____
HAIR COLOR

_____
EYE COLOR

_____
FIRST JOB

_____
CURRENT JOB

LIKES _____

_____

HOBBIES AND INTERESTS _____

_____

AWARDS AND ACHIEVEMENTS _____

_____

_____

NAME

_____
NICKNAME(S)

_____
BIRTHDAY

_____
PERSON I AM NAMED AFTER

_____
WHO I LOOK LIKE

_____
HAIR COLOR

_____
EYE COLOR

_____
FIRST JOB

_____
CURRENT JOB

LIKES _____

_____

HOBBIES AND INTERESTS _____

_____

AWARDS AND ACHIEVEMENTS _____

_____

MEMBERS OF OUR FAMILY

NAME

_____
NICKNAME(S)

_____
BIRTHDAY

_____
PERSON I AM NAMED AFTER

_____
WHO I LOOK LIKE

_____
HAIR COLOR

_____
EYE COLOR

_____
FIRST JOB

_____
CURRENT JOB

LIKES _____

_____

HOBBIES AND INTERESTS _____

_____

AWARDS AND ACHIEVEMENTS _____

_____

NAME

_____
NICKNAME(S)

_____
BIRTHDAY

_____
PERSON I AM NAMED AFTER

_____
WHO I LOOK LIKE

_____
HAIR COLOR

_____
EYE COLOR

_____
FIRST JOB

_____
CURRENT JOB

LIKES _____
_____

HOBBIES AND INTERESTS _____
_____

AWARDS AND ACHIEVEMENTS _____
_____

MEMBERS OF OUR FAMILY

NAME

_____
NICKNAME(S)

_____
PERSON I AM NAMED AFTER

_____
HAIR COLOR

_____
FIRST JOB

_____
BIRTHDAY

_____
WHO I LOOK LIKE

_____
EYE COLOR

_____
CURRENT JOB

LIKES _____

_____

HOBBIES AND INTERESTS _____

_____

AWARDS AND ACHIEVEMENTS _____

_____

NAME

NICKNAME(S)

BIRTHDAY

PERSON I AM NAMED AFTER

WHO I LOOK LIKE

HAIR COLOR

EYE COLOR

FIRST JOB

CURRENT JOB

LIKES

HOBBIES AND INTERESTS

AWARDS AND ACHIEVEMENTS

MEMBERS OF OUR FAMILY

NAME

_____
NICKNAME(S)

_____
BIRTHDAY

_____
PERSON I AM NAMED AFTER

_____
WHO I LOOK LIKE

_____
HAIR COLOR

_____
EYE COLOR

_____
FIRST JOB

_____
CURRENT JOB

LIKES _____

_____

HOBBIES AND INTERESTS _____

_____

AWARDS AND ACHIEVEMENTS _____

_____

NAME

NICKNAME(S)

BIRTHDAY

PERSON I AM NAMED AFTER

WHO I LOOK LIKE

HAIR COLOR

EYE COLOR

FIRST JOB

CURRENT JOB

LIKES _____

_____

HOBBIES AND INTERESTS _____

_____

AWARDS AND ACHIEVEMENTS _____

_____

OUR FAMILY'S ROOTS

WHERE WE COME FROM

_____

_____

_____

_____

_____

HOW WE GOT HERE

_____

_____

_____

_____

_____

_____

FAMILY HEIRLOOMS

RELATIVES WE REMEMBER MOST

ANCESTOR STORIES TO REMEMBER

FRIENDS LIKE FAMILY

The dear friends, babysitters, pets, and neighbors we love like family.

NAME

HOW WE MET _____

WHERE WE MET _____

SPECIAL TIMES WE'VE SHARED _____

_____

NAME

HOW WE MET _____

WHERE WE MET _____

SPECIAL TIMES WE'VE SHARED _____

_____

NAME

HOW WE MET _____

WHERE WE MET _____

SPECIAL TIMES WE'VE SHARED _____

_____

NAME

HOW WE MET _____

WHERE WE MET _____

SPECIAL TIMES WE'VE SHARED _____

_____

NAME

HOW WE MET _____

WHERE WE MET _____

SPECIAL TIMES WE'VE SHARED _____

_____

NAME

HOW WE MET _____

WHERE WE MET _____

SPECIAL TIMES WE'VE SHARED _____

_____

WHERE WE'VE LIVED

CURRENT ADDRESS

OUR TELEPHONE NUMBER IS

OUR NEIGHBORS ARE

QUIRKS ABOUT THE HOUSE

PREVIOUS ADDRESS

OUR TELEPHONE NUMBER WAS

OUR NEIGHBORS WERE

QUIRKS ABOUT THE HOUSE

THE CARS WE'VE DRIVEN

CAR MAKE, MODEL, AND COLOR	FOND CAR MEMORIES
WHEN WE BOUGHT IT	
WHEN WE RETIRED IT	

CAR MAKE, MODEL, AND COLOR	FOND CAR MEMORIES
WHEN WE BOUGHT IT	
WHEN WE RETIRED IT	

CAR MAKE, MODEL, AND COLOR	FOND CAR MEMORIES
WHEN WE BOUGHT IT	
WHEN WE RETIRED IT	

OUR FAMILY

CALENDAR

Use the following pages to record special
days such as birthdays, anniversaries,
and rites of passage.

JANUARY

1	17
2	18
3	19
4	20
5	21
6	22
7	23
8	24
9	25
10	26
11	27
12	28
13	29
14	30
15	31
16	

FEBRUARY

1	17
2	18
3	19
4	20
5	21
6	22
7	23
8	24
9	25
10	26
11	27
12	28
13	29
14	
15	
16	

MARCH

1	17
2	18
3	19
4	20
5	21
6	22
7	23
8	24
9	25
10	26
11	27
12	28
13	29
14	30
15	31
16	

APRIL

1	17
2	18
3	19
4	20
5	21
6	22
7	23
8	24
9	25
10	26
11	27
12	28
13	29
14	30
15	
16	

MAY

1	17
2	18
3	19
4	20
5	21
6	22
7	23
8	24
9	25
10	26
11	27
12	28
13	29
14	30
15	31
16	

JUNE

1	17
2	18
3	19
4	20
5	21
6	22
7	23
8	24
9	25
10	26
11	27
12	28
13	29
14	30
15	
16	

JULY

1	17
2	18
3	19
4	20
5	21
6	22
7	23
8	24
9	25
10	26
11	27
12	28
13	29
14	30
15	31
16	

AUGUST

1	17
2	18
3	19
4	20
5	21
6	22
7	23
8	24
9	25
10	26
11	27
12	28
13	29
14	30
15	31
16	

SEPTEMBER

1	17
2	18
3	19
4	20
5	21
6	22
7	23
8	24
9	25
10	26
11	27
12	28
13	29
14	30
15	
16	

OCTOBER

1	17
2	18
3	19
4	20
5	21
6	22
7	23
8	24
9	25
10	26
11	27
12	28
13	29
14	30
15	31
16	

NOVEMBER

1	17
2	18
3	19
4	20
5	21
6	22
7	23
8	24
9	25
10	26
11	27
12	28
13	29
14	30
15	
16	

DECEMBER

1	17
2	18
3	19
4	20
5	21
6	22
7	23
8	24
9	25
10	26
11	27
12	28
13	29
14	30
15	31
16	

OUR FAMILY
CUSTOMS

HOLIDAY TRADITIONS

HOLIDAY	CUSTOMS AND TRADITIONS
WHERE WE CELEBRATE	
WHO WE CELEBRATE WITH	

HOLIDAY	CUSTOMS AND TRADITIONS
WHERE WE CELEBRATE	
WHO WE CELEBRATE WITH	

HOLIDAY

CUSTOMS AND TRADITIONS

WHERE WE CELEBRATE

WHO WE CELEBRATE WITH

HOLIDAY

CUSTOMS AND TRADITIONS

WHERE WE CELEBRATE

WHO WE CELEBRATE WITH

HOLIDAY TRADITIONS

HOLIDAY

WHERE WE CELEBRATE

WHO WE CELEBRATE WITH

CUSTOMS AND TRADITIONS

HOLIDAY

WHERE WE CELEBRATE

WHO WE CELEBRATE WITH

CUSTOMS AND TRADITIONS

HOLIDAY

WHERE WE CELEBRATE

WHO WE CELEBRATE WITH

CUSTOMS AND TRADITIONS

HOLIDAY

WHERE WE CELEBRATE

WHO WE CELEBRATE WITH

CUSTOMS AND TRADITIONS

FAMILY REUNIONS

WHEN _____

WHERE _____

WHO CAME _____

_____

_____

WHAT WE DID _____

_____

_____

_____

_____

WHEN _____

WHERE _____

WHO CAME _____

_____

_____

WHAT WE DID _____

_____

_____

_____

_____

WHEN _____

WHERE _____

WHO CAME _____

_____

_____

WHAT WE DID _____

_____

_____

_____

_____

WHEN _____

WHERE _____

WHO CAME _____

_____

_____

WHAT WE DID _____

_____

_____

_____

_____

EVERYDAY RITUALS

MORNING RITUALS _____

_____

_____

_____

_____

_____

MEALTIME RITUALS _____

_____

_____

_____

_____

_____

BEDTIME RITUALS _____

_____

_____

_____

_____

_____

WEEKEND RITUALS _____

_____

_____

_____

_____

_____

BIRTHDAY RITUALS _____

_____

_____

_____

_____

_____

SEASONAL RITUALS _____

_____

_____

_____

_____

_____

RULES WE LIVE BY

The rules, chores, and practices that are part of our everyday lives.

CHERISHED ADVICE

The important values and words of wisdom that hold true.

_____

_____

_____

_____

_____

_____

_____

_____

_____

_____

_____

_____

_____

_____

_____

_____

_____

_____

_____

FAMILY

FAVORITES

❧ THINGS WE LOVE ❧

OUR FAVORITE MOVIES

OUR FAVORITE TELEVISION SHOWS

OUR FAVORITE BOOKS

OUR FAVORITE MUSICALS

OUR FAVORITE SONGS

OUR FAVORITE MUSEUMS

OUR FAVORITE RESTAURANTS

OUR FAVORITE CAR RIDE GAMES

OUR FAVORITE PLAYGROUNDS AND PARKS

OUR FAVORITE DAY TRIPS

OUR FAVORITE BOARD GAMES

OUR FAVORITE JOKES

MORE THINGS WE LOVE

FAMILY EXPRESSIONS AND PRIVATE JOKES

Our favorite dinner table lines and jokes that only we understand.

FAVORITE FAMILY STORIES

The legends, lore, and infamous tales we love to retell.

_____

_____

_____

_____

_____

_____

_____

_____

_____

_____

_____

_____

_____

_____

_____

_____

_____

_____

_____

FAVORITE FAMILY STORIES

_____

_____

_____

_____

_____

_____

_____

_____

_____

_____

_____

_____

_____

_____

_____

_____

_____

_____

_____

_____

FAVORITE FAMILY STORIES

UNFORGETTABLE RECIPES

RECIPE

FROM THE KITCHEN OF

INGREDIENTS	DIRECTIONS

RECIPE

FROM THE KITCHEN OF

INGREDIENTS	DIRECTIONS

RECIPE

FROM THE KITCHEN OF

INGREDIENTS	DIRECTIONS

RECIPE

FROM THE KITCHEN OF

INGREDIENTS	DIRECTIONS

UNFORGETTABLE RECIPES

RECIPE _____

FROM THE KITCHEN OF _____

INGREDIENTS	DIRECTIONS

RECIPE _____

FROM THE KITCHEN OF _____

INGREDIENTS	DIRECTIONS

RECIPE

FROM THE KITCHEN OF

INGREDIENTS	DIRECTIONS

RECIPE

FROM THE KITCHEN OF

INGREDIENTS	DIRECTIONS

VACATIONS

❧ FAMILY VACATIONS ☙

WHEN _____

WHERE WE WENT _____

WHAT WE DID _____

_____

_____

HAPPIEST MEMORY _____

_____

MORE STORIES FROM THE TRIP _____

_____

_____

_____

WHEN _____

WHERE WE WENT _____

WHAT WE DID _____

_____

_____

HAPPIEST MEMORY _____

_____

MORE STORIES FROM THE TRIP _____

_____

_____

WHEN _____

WHERE WE WENT _____

WHAT WE DID _____

_____

_____

HAPPIEST MEMORY _____

_____

MORE STORIES FROM THE TRIP _____

_____

_____

_____

WHEN _____

WHERE WE WENT _____

WHAT WE DID _____

_____

_____

HAPPIEST MEMORY _____

_____

MORE STORIES FROM THE TRIP _____

_____

_____

_____

FAMILY VACATIONS

WHEN _____

WHERE WE WENT _____

WHAT WE DID _____

_____

_____

HAPPIEST MEMORY _____

_____

MORE STORIES FROM THE TRIP _____

_____

_____

_____

WHEN _____

WHERE WE WENT _____

WHAT WE DID _____

_____

_____

HAPPIEST MEMORY _____

_____

MORE STORIES FROM THE TRIP _____

_____

_____

_____

WHEN _____

WHERE WE WENT _____

WHAT WE DID _____

_____

_____

HAPPIEST MEMORY _____

_____

MORE STORIES FROM THE TRIP _____

_____

_____

_____

WHEN _____

WHERE WE WENT _____

WHAT WE DID _____

_____

_____

HAPPIEST MEMORY _____

_____

MORE STORIES FROM THE TRIP _____

_____

_____

_____

FAMILY VACATIONS

WHEN _____

WHERE WE WENT _____

WHAT WE DID _____

_____

_____

HAPPIEST MEMORY _____

_____

MORE STORIES FROM THE TRIP_____

_____

_____

_____

WHEN _____

WHERE WE WENT _____

WHAT WE DID _____

_____

_____

HAPPIEST MEMORY _____

_____

MORE STORIES FROM THE TRIP_____

_____

_____

WHEN _____

WHERE WE WENT _____

WHAT WE DID _____

_____

_____

HAPPIEST MEMORY _____

_____

MORE STORIES FROM THE TRIP _____

_____

_____

_____

WHEN _____

WHERE WE WENT _____

WHAT WE DID _____

_____

_____

HAPPIEST MEMORY _____

_____

MORE STORIES FROM THE TRIP _____

_____

_____

_____

WHERE WE'VE TRAVELED

Mark off where we've explored together.

MORE MEMORIES, MOMENTS, AND MILESTONES TO REMEMBER

_____

_____

_____

_____

_____

_____

_____

_____

_____

_____

_____

_____

_____

_____

_____

_____

_____

_____

_____

ISBN: 978-1-4521-3546-5

Manufactured in China

Design by Anne Kenady
Illustrations by Minna So

10 9 8 7 6 5 4 3 2

Chronicle Books LLC
680 Second Street
San Francisco, California 94107
www.chroniclebooks.com